# Dear Tabby

OTHER BOOKS BY LEIGH W. RUTLEDGE

*A Cat's Little Instruction Book*

*Cat Love Letters*

*It Seemed Like a Good Idea at the Time*

*The Lefthander's Guide to Life*

# Dear Tabby

Leigh W. Rutledge

A DUTTON BOOK

DUTTON
Published by the Penguin Group
Penguin Books USA Inc., 375 Hudson Street,
New York, New York 10014, U.S.A.
Penguin Books Ltd, 27 Wrights Lane, London W8 5TZ, England
Penguin Books Australia Ltd, Ringwood, Victoria, Australia
Penguin Books Canada Ltd, 10 Alcorn Avenue,
Toronto, Ontario, Canada M4V 3B2
Penguin Books (N.Z.) Ltd, 182–190 Wairau Road,
Auckland 10, New Zealand

Penguin Books Ltd, Registered Offices:
Harmondsworth, Middlesex, England

First published by Dutton, an imprint of Dutton Signet,
a division of Penguin Books USA Inc.
Distributed in Canada by McClelland & Stewart Inc.

First Printing, February, 1995
10 9 8 7 6 5 4 3 2 1

 REGISTERED TRADEMARK—MARCA REGISTRADA

LIBRARY OF CONGRESS CATALOGING-IN-PUBLICATION DATA
Rutledge, Leigh W.
Dear Tabby / Leigh W. Rutledge.
p.   cm.
ISBN 0-525-93944-X
1. Cats—Humor.   2. Advice columns—Humor.   I. Title.
PN6231.C23R88   1995
818'.5402—dc20                                94-33413
                                                        CIP

Printed in the United States of America
Set in Glypha Light and Deepdene Italic
Designed by Eve L. Kirch

PUBLISHER'S NOTE
This is a work of fiction. Names, characters, places, and incidents either are
the products of the author's imagination or are used fictitiously, and any
resemblance to actual persons, living or dead, events, or locales is entirely
coincidental.

This book is printed on acid-free paper.

∞

"Dear Tabby" finds herself in the somewhat awkward position of wishing to dedicate this volume to a human. However, this book—a compilation of the best letters from her column— owes its very existence to her longtime editor and friend, Peter Borland. My sincere appreciation to him—and my apologies to any of my faithful readers who find the idea of dedicating a book to a human distasteful.

*TABBY* 🐾

Dear Tabby,

Do cats have to obey the speed limit? My friend Ding-Dong says that if you run down the street faster than 25 mph, you're breaking the law and you could theoretically be ticketed. What do you say?

—A Reader in Dubuque

*DEAR DUBUQUE,*

*I say that whoever named your friend Ding-Dong was an unusually prescient individual. The only time a cat would have to worry about the speed limit would be in the unlikely event he was driving an automobile—and then the speed limit would probably be one of the least of his worries.*

Dear Tabby,

My best friend, Snowball, is head over heels in love with an old throw pillow. He sleeps with it all night, rubs his head against it all day—the other day he was wrestling on the floor with it. He's throwing his poor little kitty life away on this pillow. What can I do to help straighten him out?

—A Desperate Friend

*DEAR DESPERATE FRIEND,*

*Stay out of it. You must never make a cat choose between you and his pillow—the pillow will always win.*

Dear Tabby,

This may seem like a stupid question, but I'm only twelve weeks old and the humans I live with are always telling me, "Remember, curiosity killed the cat. . . ." No matter what I do, it's always, "Curiosity killed the cat. Curiosity killed the cat. . . ." Is there any truth at all to this?

—Curious in Cleveland

*DEAR CURIOUS,*

*How many times have you heard a human confidently remark, "Look before you leap," one minute, only to say, with equal confidence, "He who hesitates is lost," the next? Humans adore quaint sayings, and it hardly seems to matter to them that most of these simple homilies contradict one another. Truisms are like toads—they all look good until you sink your teeth into one. In regard to curiosity, all I can say is never, ever believe any propaganda about the supposedly lethal nature of inquisitiveness. As a cat, you must revel in your curiosity—about everyone and everything. Curiosity never killed anyone, not a single kitty. Complacency, on the other hand, can steal your soul.*

Dear Tabby,

Do cats go to heaven? Last Sunday morning I overheard a minister on TV claim that only humans go to heaven; he implied that other animals don't even have souls. This really depressed me. Please, Tabby, what's the truth? If cats aren't allowed into heaven, where *do* we go?

—In Limbo in Lima, Ohio

*Dear in Limbo,*

*Heaven is reserved for anyone who generously brings comfort and happiness to others and fills their lives with peace and love. As such, most cats will almost certainly go to heaven. On the other hand, the minister you overheard on television may have a shock in store for him when he dies.*

Dear Tabby,

What is love? I keep thinking I can live without it, that it shouldn't be important at all. But, then I see the tomcat down the street, and all I do is long for him—the smell of his neck, the touch of his chin against mine. I live for the sight of his slim body as he trots down the sidewalk on a summer morning. One part of me wants to be completely free, to roam the world without wanting anything. But it's hopeless. Why do I ache this way even though every cell in my feline brain says not to bother with love at all?

—Troubled in Santa Barbara

*Dear Troubled,*

*Ambivalence is a natural part of all romantic encounters. But, inevitably, you must give in to your heart to be happy. Next time that little tomcat trots by, throw yourself on the sidewalk and start rolling around in front of him. It won't take long for your doubts to disappear—at least for the afternoon.*

Dear Tabby,

Is it normal for a male cat to still want sex after ten?

—An Exhausted Mate

*DEAR EXHAUSTED*,

*Yes. And in the mornings and the afternoons, too.*

Dear Tabby,

I am a human writing to you in utter desperation. Recently I adopted a two-year-old male cat from the local animal shelter. In just two weeks he's repaid my generosity by yanking down all the living room curtains, scattering my pens all over the house, shedding hair on my best clothes, and to beat everything he regularly coughs up fur balls in the middle of the bathtub. I also suspect him of snatching dollar bills from my dresser. He's one of the cutest cats I've ever owned, but he's so rambunctious and full of mischief it's killing me. On top of that, I already have two other cats who used to sleep all day and never gave me any trouble; now the three of them tear through the house like drunken tigers. I scream at them constantly, and I've started whacking them all regularly with a ruler to calm them down, but nothing has an effect. Oh, Tabby—what can I do to make my house a happy home again?

—Fed Up

*DEAR FED UP,*

*You could leave.*

Dear Tabby,

I am utterly miserable, and I have no one else to turn to. I am an old cat, and I have lived all my life in the alleys. I've been kicked, I've been beaten, I've been in so many fights I've lost track of them all. I've had people throw garbage at me, I've had them go out of their way to try and hit me with their cars. I no longer have any whiskers, and I have only one ear. I barely have any tail to speak of.

My problem is that I am desperately in love with the most beautiful Angora cat you have ever seen. I've spent entire mornings watching her as she suns herself in her yard. I've waited by her house for hours just to catch a glimpse of her nibbling the front grass. Whenever I see her I feel young and happy and handsome. Only later, when I'm alone, do I remember who I really am again. Oh, Tabby, what should I do? The thought of introducing myself to her paralyzes me. I know there's no hope she could ever fall in love with me. I also know I can never forget her. Please, *please* help me.

—Wretched in Boston

## DEAR WRETCHED,

Why, oh why, have you chosen this moment to forget that cats, perhaps more than any other creatures, are indifferent to physical appearances? If your meow is still sweet and sincere, if your soul is loyal, if you have a good heart—what else matters? Pursue your beautiful Angora idol. She may be sitting in her garden at this very moment wondering why no one ever comes to play with her. Beauty is, after all, no guarantee of bliss. Go to her at once. You'll regret it forever if you don't, no matter what the outcome is.

🐾

Dear Tabby,

For years I used to fight with the cat next door. The reasons never seemed to matter much: a grasshopper we both spotted at the same time, an unpleasant hiss shot in one or the other's direction. Then this spring, all of that suddenly changed, and I'm confused. My whiskers still shake when I see him, but I don't think it's anger anymore. And he still wants to bite me, but not in the same places as before. The other day he came charging up to me but at the last minute, instead of swatting me, he just started to make loud trilling noises and tried to rub his head against my shoulders. What's up? How could this be happening to us? Help!

—Thunderstruck in Omaha

## Dear Thunderstruck,

*Never be concerned if an enemy suddenly turns into a lover. It happens all the time. At least it means fewer scratches and abscesses. If you're truly worried, just remember: with time, lots of lovers turn back into enemies.*

Dear Tabby,

What do humans think about when they're sitting around all day staring at the walls? My friend Maybelline says they're probably daydreaming about suppertime. I say they're just plain stupid and nothing much goes on in their heads. Who's right?

—Just Wondering

*DEAR WONDERING,*

*Although they sometimes appear to be in a total stupor, especially when they're in front of the television, humans actually have fairly active imaginations. However, most of their fantasies are restricted to simple daydreams about food, sex, and telling off other humans.*

Dear Tabby,

The woman I lived with for sixteen years recently died. She was the most wonderful human I've ever known. I miss her so much I sometimes feel like I'm going to die, too. She never hit me, never yelled at me. The house was always full of kitty treats. We spent many happy winter days together curled up on the sofa reading, or napping while the snow fell, or watching old movies. During the spring and summer, I would help her plant her garden—and sometimes I'd doze off in the shade, content with the knowledge that she was always there and all I had to do was open my eyes to see her planting her flowers. She was old, and all her friends had died, except for me. We were inseparable. I would give anything now to hear her call my name, or feel her scratching my head. I am all alone, Tabby. What should I do now? I have nowhere to go. I think I will probably be put to sleep. Can you help?

—Hopeless in Chicago

## DEAR HOPELESS,

There are humans who touch our lives so deeply, so completely, that the loss of them seems unendurable. I know of cats who, having lost a human companion, simply wandered into the basement and refused all food and water until they, too, finally died. But how wonderful for you to have had sixteen years with a human you cherished! And how wonderful for her to have had you in her life. It would have been better had she made some arrangements for you in her will—I'm afraid the world isn't kind to elderly cats who survive their human companions. You can stay where you are and take your chances (admittedly poor) with her heirs. Or you can look for the first opportunity to escape and then take your chances on the street. You may even find a kind stranger who will take you in. It won't be the same as it was—but then nothing ever is. My thoughts are with you.

Dear Tabby,

I'm sick and tired of you always bashing humans in your column. Either we're stupid and lazy, or we're selfish and narcissistic. If it weren't for humans, where do you think your food would come from? Who do you think would make Ping-Pong balls and catnip toys and scratching posts? Certainly not cats! You're all too busy chasing your tails and torturing houseplants! Your oft-stated distaste for humans seems to me the most gratuitous form of sneering, all the more offensive since you know damn well we can't retaliate without looking like bullies!

—Human and Proud in Tulsa


*Dear Human and Proud,*

*How many times have you seen cats run by each other's homes and fire guns at the windows? When was the last time you saw a mob of cats, armed to the teeth, marching down the street for the sole purpose of annihilating the cats in another neighborhood? It seems to me that if humans spent more time chasing their tails and playing with their houseplants, the world would be a saner place.*

Dear Tabby,

The love of my life is a three-year-old Persian, but she's the vainest cat I've ever known. If a single hair is out of place, she immediately stops whatever she's doing and starts licking herself over and over. It doesn't matter if we're chasing each other around the lilacs or trying to make love in the moonlight— her first priority is always how she looks. My mother warned me about this when I first told her I was dating a Persian. What do you think?

—Always Waiting

## DEAR ALWAYS WAITING,

Persians are, by nature, incredibly self-absorbed. If you can overcome playing second fiddle to all her narcissistic impulses, fine. (You might consider taking up a hobby, like world travel, to kill the time while she's cleaning herself.) If not, find yourself a nice short-haired beauty who'll find you more fascinating than her coiffure.

Dear Tabby,

Recently I moved in with a human family, and after several days of debate on the subject, they have decided to name me Meow Tse-tung. They think this is the funniest thing anyone ever thought of, and they can't even say my name without rolling on the floor like lunatics. All day long it's "Meow Tse-tung, Meow Tse-tung," followed by fits of uncontrollable laughter. Sometimes they even pull on the corners of their eyes to make them slanted, and then march around the room reciting my name in a singsongy Chinese accent. I've tried to explain to them that for years my name has been Bridget but, alas, no one pays any attention to me. Is there anything I can do, short of running off?

—*Not* Meow Tse-tung

*DEAR NOT,*

It is one of the constant perils of cat life that most humans have no idea what we're saying and little interest in learning. Gestures must, therefore, speak louder than meows. Next time—and every time—they call you that name, simply jump on top of the TV and pee down the back of it. This will certainly get their attention and may alert them to the need to rename you. While it's doubtful they'll ever figure out you want to be called Bridget, they'll hopefully find something better than Meow Tsetung, although it's hard to imagine that anyone who pulls their eyes into a slant and talks in a fake Chinese accent is going to get the hint about anything ever.

Dear Tabby,

For weeks now I've been watching this little red-breasted robin who sits every morning outside my kitchen window. She really makes me smack my lips. At first I thought I was only hungry—now I realize it's love. What can I do to convince her I'm sincere?

—Bird-Watching in Baltimore

*DEAR BIRD-WATCHING,*

*Have all your teeth pulled.*

Dear Tabby,

Why do they only make cat food in the same old stupid flavors—chicken, beef, and tuna—year after year? Why don't they make cat food in the flavors we *really* want: "Moth Stew," "Country Lizard," and "Mouse Heads Surprise"?

—Hungry in the Hamptons

*DEAR HUNGRY IN THE HAMPTONS,*

*Because I suspect most humans would lose their lunch before they could get the cans from the shelf and into the shopping cart. Humans can be very touchy about this sort of thing, and although I did forward your letter to several pet-food companies, I wouldn't look for "Savory Bug Platter" or "Squirrels with Gravy" anytime soon.*

Dear Tabby,

I have been living for five years with the most wonderful, loyal tomcat in the world. I'm not the jealous type, but last Friday night he came home late with suspicious little nibble marks all over his neck and ears. When I asked him how he got them, he claimed he was attacked by a flock of vicious woodpeckers. At first I believed him. But then it occurred to me: birds don't fly at night, do they?

—Skeptical

*DEAR SKEPTICAL,*

*Some "birds" do indeed fly at night, but they usually have names like "Muffin," "Whiskers," and "Miss Kitty." Next time he comes home with someone else's nibble marks all over him, tell him you're going to fly the coop unless he settles down.*

Dear Tabby,

I know you normally don't publish letters from dogs, but is it really true that there's more than one way to skin a cat? Please be as specific as possible.

—Just Doing a Little Research in Seattle

*Dear Doing Research,*

*Certainly, it is. However, first you'd have to catch one, and for a dog with your brains that would probably require dumb luck. It also assumes you're smart enough to tell a cat from an old shoe—something hounds like you often have trouble with. Oh, you are just too, too transparent. Actually, I only published this letter to show my readers once again why the phrase "gone to the dogs" universally refers to depravity, decline, and stupidity.*

Dear Tabby,

Recently you printed a letter from a Baltimore cat who had fallen in love with a bird. From your flippant reply, I gather you think the relationship is a silly one. I'll have you know that for three years now I've had a very happy relationship with a duck. Sure, some cats think it's odd. And there's been a lot of clucking from *her* fine-feathered friends. But her quacks are the closest thing to heaven I've ever experienced, and love is love no matter what form it takes, and there's so little of it in the world I'm surprised you'd stoop to condemn it. I think "Bird-Watching in Baltimore" deserved a more considerate and thoughtful response.

—Just Ducky in Detroit


*DEAR JUST DUCKY,*

*Apparently, I struck a nerve. I heard from dozens of lovesick cats smitten with birds, skunks, rabbits, and even a python—and almost all of them took me to task. My response to "Bird-Watching in Baltimore" was only meant to underscore the potential problems when different species become romantically involved—especially when they occupy different niches in the food chain.*

Dear Tabby,

I was incensed by your reply to "Bird-Watching in Baltimore" a few weeks ago. Why were you so coy? Why didn't you just condemn him outright? You do a real disservice when you promote the kind of love espoused by perverted cats who take a romantic hankering to birds in their gardens. I'm sure I speak for many when I say your column that morning made me want to heave fur balls all over the kitchen counter. Perhaps you should take another look at your birdbrained notions.

—Disgusted in Dallas

*DEAR DISGUSTED,*

*Your letter certainly disproves the idea that all cats have nine lives. Some cats don't have even one. I hope you get one soon.*

Dear Tabby,

Thank you, thank you, *thank you* for publishing the letter from the cat who'd been named Meow Tse-tung by insensitive humans. I know just how miserable she feels. For several years now, *I've* had to cope with the name Claws von Bulow. The humans I live with find the name irresistibly funny and take every opportunity to interject it into conversation with visitors. Please, Tabby, let's get the message out there: keep cats' names simple, descriptive, and charming. (And *please*—avoid naming cats after defendants in criminal trials.)

—C.V.B.

*DEAR C.V.B.,*

*You aren't the only one I heard from on this topic, not by a long shot. Read on.*

🐾

Dear Tabby,

I know just how Meow Tse-tung feels. My owner named me Evita Purron, and used to go around singing "Don't Cry for Me, Argentina" every time she picked me up. . . .

Dear Tabby,

So Meow Tse-tung thinks *she* has it bad? How about living with the name John Paws II? Whenever my owner's friends come over, they genuflect in front of me and kiss my paw. They think this is quite funny. . . .

Dear Tabby,

How would *you* like to go through life with the name Ling Gweenie?

Dear Tabby,

I've had a succession of *four* names in the last year, *all from the same family.* First, they called me Miss Demeanor, but when that was no longer funny they tried Princess Marsha Mellow. After that, it was Kitty Mae Knott. Then, it was Duchess Purranha. Finally they got bored with the whole thing (and me), and now they just call me Cat. . . .

Dear Tabby,

At least Meow Tse-tung *has* a name. I've lived with the same family for two years, and they *still* haven't given me a name. They just holler out, "Hey, you!" "Come here, you dirty little fuzzball!" The vet keeps pushing them to give me a name, for his files if nothing else, but whenever he brings it up they just blink at him as if they were listening to a lecture on astrophysics. . . .

Dear Tabby,

I know just what Meow Tse-tung is talking about. I live in Marin County and was given the name Armistead Meowpin nine years ago. I guess I shouldn't complain too much. At least I was named after someone with *talent*. . . .

## DEAR READERS,

If it's any consolation, humans also curse their own children with prankish names. Witness a young woman I recently met whose name was Sandy Shore. Or another woman whose parents couldn't resist christening her Anna Gramm. Letters on the subject of stupid names poured in from cats all over the country. I heard from a General Purrshing, a King Furrdinand, a Siamese named Tai Won On, and half a dozen poor cats cursed with the name Santa Claws. Gizmo is a name thrust on countless cats unlucky enough to have been born in 1984. And I was amazed by the number of animals who have been named after brand-name products: Burger King, Pepsi, Endust, and Clorox.

Obviously, this is a chronic problem that isn't going to be solved overnight, and the solution I suggested to Meow Tse-tung won't work for everybody. Perhaps just bringing it to light will help correct it—though (the eternal pessimist) I have grave doubts.

Dear Tabby,

Is it true that the ancient Egyptians used to mummify their cats? Is anyone still doing this today? I would much rather be mummified than buried in the flower bed out back. I think it would be much more dignified, don't you? Can you tell me how much it would cost, and whether a nice little sarcophagus would also be provided for me?

—Cleo in Memphis

*DEAR CLEO,*

*It's true the ancient Egyptians used to mummify their cats. However, I have no idea whether anyone's currently offering this practice to modern kitties. If they were, the cost would probably vary widely, depending on what little extras you requested, such as whether or not you wanted your attendants buried alive with you. Finishing touches —such as a pyramid over your remains—might make the cost prohibitive. My own feeling is that "the flower bed out back" is a pretty good deal: there's always been something comforting about returning to the raw earth and knowing that one's molecules might one day see sunlight again in the form of a rose or a daffodil.*

Dear Tabby,

I was sitting in the road the other day minding my own business when a car full of teenagers drove by honking their horn and screaming, "Turn up your hearing aid, cat!" Please, Tabby, tell your readers how painful these words are and how it cuts like a knife to have one's inadequacies hollered out for all the neighbors to hear. After all, the boys had only to go around me.

—A Little Hard of Hearing

## *Dear Hard of Hearing,*

*It would've been a lot more painful if they had run over you. I don't think you have much to complain about—teenage boys who drive around cats in the road (whatever their remarks as they pass) are candidates for sainthood.*

29

Dear Tabby,

How many cats would it take, lined up tail to nose, to reach from here to the moon? I don't know why I keep thinking about this question, but I'm trying to get an idea of just how far away places like the moon really are. Thanks.

—Staggered by the Immensity of It All

*Dear Staggered,*

*Assuming a distance from the earth to the moon of approximately 235,000 miles, and assuming the average cat is roughly 26 inches in length from the tip of its nose to the end of its tail, it would take nearly 572,692,000 cats laid end to end to reach to the moon. It would, of course, take about 300 million more of them if they were all Manxes.*

Dear Tabby,

My cat stares at me all the time and I don't know what to do about it. She obviously thinks I'm up to something. I swear I'm not. What should I do?

—An Innocent Man

## DEAR INNOCENT,

Cats stare at all sorts of things all the time, and the secret is not to take it personally. On the other hand, they're expert judges of character, and it's possible you're harboring a guilty secret and she's onto it. Perhaps you should turn yourself in to the police, just to make sure you haven't done something wrong. If you really are innocent, they'll let you go eventually.

🐾

Dear Tabby,

Please settle an argument I've been having with the cat across the street—is it proper to wear a white collar after Labor Day?

—Fashion-Conscious in Phoenix

*DEAR FASHION-CONSCIOUS,*

Only if you're a priest.

Dear Tabby,

What do you do when the tomcat you love suddenly trots in one afternoon and announces he's leaving you and the kittens for someone else? What's even worse, the "someone else" is a schnauzer named Gretchen! How am I supposed to explain to the little ones that Daddy deserted them for a dog? What should I tell my friends? How can I live with this? What does a dog have that I don't?

—Abandoned in Albuquerque

*DEAR ABANDONED,*

*To answer your questions in order: 1) Don't even try to explain the specifics to your little ones. Contrary to popular belief, it isn't essential that offspring know everything about their parents. 2) Don't tell your friends anything—trust me, they've already heard. 3) Count your blessings—a cat who'd fall in love with a schnauzer named Gretchen is no role model for kittens. 4) Big ears, bad breath, and an irresistible urge to become romantically attached to the legs of strangers.*

Dear Tabby,

How should I tell the kitten next door that I love her? We're both about the same age, and I haven't had any previous experience with this sort of thing (I presume she hasn't either). My biggest fear is that I'll make a fool of myself and she'll scurry away convinced I'm the wrong cat for her.

—Lovesick in Stockton

*DEAR LOVESICK IN STOCKTON,*

*There are many ways you can tell her you love her. You can share some of your dinner with her. You can share one of your toys with her. You can take her for strolls in the moonlight. You can even, when you're sitting together in the flower bed, give one of her ears a quick furtive lick; but only so long as you tell her, "Oh, I'm sorry—I thought you had a mosquito on your ear." (She'll understand it's a charming lie.) After a while, you'll probably have some idea whether she's receptive to your feelings—and if she is, it'll be impossible to make a fool of yourself. "I love you" is what she'll be longing to hear.*

Dear Tabby,

I constantly get food stuck in my whiskers and have sometimes gone around for hours with some little morsel stuck to me before a friend was kind enough to point it out. Is there a way to avoid this embarrassment to begin with?

—A Diner in Danbury

*DEAR DINER IN DANBURY,*

*Some cats tend to shove their entire noses into the food dish when they eat and wind up carrying much of the meal all over their faces when they're done. Always nibble your food slowly—snatch a bite with your teeth first, and then pull away from the bowl to savor it. The alternative, of course, is dry food—or to dunk your head in the toilet for a few seconds after every meal.*

Dear Tabby,

When humans tell me, "There should be a law against being so cute," are they serious? Is anyone actually trying to pass such a law?

—Nervous on Nantucket

*DEAR NERVOUS ON NANTUCKET,*

*No, they aren't serious. No, no one's trying to pass such a law. Your cuteness is safe.*

Dear Tabby,

Where do you stand on the issue of body piercings for cats?

—Tempted in Tampa

*Dear Tempted,*

*I stand out of the way of anyone with a needle in his hand—that's where I stand. You don't make it clear from your signature whether you're a human tempted to do it to your cat, or a cat tempted to do it to yourself. If the former, you're a sadist; if the latter, you're an imbecile. The only thing piercing about a cat should be its gaze.*

Dear Tabby,

Several months ago you published a letter from an alley cat, "Wretched in Boston," who was in love with a beautiful Angora cat he thought was unattainable. You advised him to go to her immediately and confess his adoration, no matter what the outcome was. Oh, Tabby, *how can I ever thank you? I* am that Angora cat. "Wretched in Boston" introduced himself shortly after reading your reply. He came into my garden, shy and skittish and watchful—and almost immediately I knew I'd been waiting there for him all my life. We are now devoted to each other, walking through the grass on a sunny day, sleeping by the fire at night, chasing each other around the dining room furniture. He's the most caring and charming cat I've ever known. Sometimes he still cries out in his sleep, an echo of his life in the alleys. And I still look out the window with an occasional feeling of melancholy (I still re-member all those lonely days in my garden). But we have each other now. Thank you, Tabby, for chang-ing two lonely cats' lives forever.

—Overjoyed in Boston

*DEAR OVERJOYED IN BOSTON,*

*Some letters need no reply. This is one of them. My best wishes for all good things for both of you always.*

Dear Tabby,

What would be a good New Year's resolution for a cat? I can't think of anything this year. All the old ones I've ever made—not clawing the furniture, not teasing the dog, not using the flower bed as a litter box—I've always wound up breaking. Do you have a good one for me?

—A Reader in Vermont

*DEAR VERMONT,*

*Yes, I have two. Don't make resolutions you can't possibly keep. Don't imitate inane human customs.*

Dear Tabby,

When is it proper to sniff a total stranger?

—Miss Daisy in Dartmouth

*DEAR MISS DAISY,*

*Whenever one's handy.*

Dear Tabby,

I've been living for six weeks now with a lovely four-year-old Manx, and I adore almost everything about her. My problem is that she only likes to be amorous in the most peculiar places. Last week, it was on top of a mailbox. The week before that, it was on the front seat of a UPS truck—while the driver was making deliveries! Recently, she's been eyeing the little floating raft in a neighbor's pool, and I can tell what's on her mind. Whenever we're at home, she's not in a romantic mood at all. Am I the only tomcat with this problem?

—Bewildered in Biloxi


*DEAR BEWILDERED,*

*Your sweetheart obviously enjoys a little danger to spice up her passion. So long as she's not suggesting anything potentially injurious—making love while balanced on telephone wires, or on top of a fast-moving car—it's harmless. You should be grateful to have found a kitty with such a sense of adventure and so much imagination. Your "problem" isn't common, but I bet there are a lot of tomcats out there who wish it were.*

🐾

Dear Tabby,

What can you say about a cat who's more comfortable with raccoons than he is with cats? One of my kittens from the last litter wants nothing to do with other cats but spends all of his time with a bunch of raccoons that live near here. It's got me worried. He's so friendly with them I think he's turning into one of them. What kind of cat is it who spends all his time socializing with raccoons?

—Aghast in Augusta

*DEAR AGHAST,*

*A raccoonteur.*

Dear Tabby,

Now I've heard everything. A cat in Memphis wants to be mummified? Another, in Florida, is curious about body piercings? What's next—liposuction and tummy tucks for cats, or maybe cryogenic freezing so some kitties can have their heads resuscitated in the twenty-second century! Don't some cats have anything better to do with their time than worry about these things? I'm sorry, Tabby, but your column is really becoming a refuse heap for all the feline flotsam out there. Enough already!

—Sick and Tired in Boise

P.S. I bet you won't have the guts to publish this.

*DEAR SICK AND TIRED,*

*Don't some cats have anything better to do with their time than write letters complaining about cats they think have nothing better to do with their time? Who are you to decide what other cats should be worried about? It's you who required a certain kind of "guts"—or should I say nerve—to write such a foolish letter.*

Dear Tabby,

Is there a way to keep from coughing up fur balls at all the wrong times? No matter how hard I try to control it, I seem to cough them up at the most inopportune moments. It doesn't matter whether I'm in the middle of trying to impress the female cat next door, or running from a dog, or stalking a bird—fur balls keep popping out of me. Is there any cure?

—Coughing One Up Right Now


*DEAR COUGHING ONE UP,*

*Only one—death.*

Dear Tabby,

Why don't cats laugh? My cat never laughs, regardless of what anyone says or does. I've even hidden behind a door sometimes to watch and see if she laughs when I'm out of the room. She doesn't. I'm worried.

—Concerned in Newport, Rhode Island

## DEAR CONCERNED IN NEWPORT,

*Who says cats don't laugh? They just don't make fools of themselves by rolling out of their chairs, slapping their knees, guffawing out loud, and poking the cat next to them in the ribs. Cats prefer to laugh as Queen Victoria did: in regal silence.*

Dear Tabby,

Several cats I know have recently taken up genealogy and it seems I can't go anywhere anymore without hearing who's related to Morris the Cat or who's descended from a cat Winston Churchill once kept as a pet. The whole thing is tiresome beyond belief. Don't you agree it's rude for cats to brag about their lineage?

—An Ordinary Cat in Toronto

## Dear Ordinary in Toronto,

It's not only rude; it's pointless. Given the complicated soup of wandering tomcats and alley-cat maidens from which almost all of us were conceived, I sincerely doubt that any of us can trace with certainty his or her connection to Morris or Socks or a kitten Marcel Proust once played with as a child. It's the legacy of love and happiness we leave after us—not the chance matings that preceded us—that should concern every well-brought-up and intelligent creature.

Dear Tabby,

Is it true that the best way to catch a tomcat is to rub catnip all over your fur and then stand slightly upwind from him?

—Willing to Try Anything

*DEAR WILLING TO TRY ANYTHING,*

*Only if you want him to tackle you, drag you all over the yard, toss you in the air, chew on you, bat you around the lawn, and then fall asleep.*

Dear Tabby,

There are mice all over my house, but my cat refuses to catch a single one of them. At first I wondered if she was deaf and didn't hear them, but then I saw her ears prick up yesterday while one went scurrying through the walls. Tell me, are there cats who are conscientious objectors?

—A Puzzled Human in Peoria

*DEAR PUZZLED,*

*No, but there are cats who object to being thought of as mousetraps with paws. Call an exterminator.*

Dear Tabby,

My name is June McPhee and I'm an eleven-year-old girl and I have a little kitten named Precious Topaz who was named that because she is the most precious little thing in the world and she has the biggest eyes that look just like big round jewels. She's celebrating her six-month birthday soon and I haven't the faintest idea what to get her. I've thought of all sorts of pretty things for her but nothing seems right and when I asked my mother about it she said that maybe a nice little rubber ball would do, but that seems so common, doesn't it to you? My father didn't say anything, he just sat in his big chair reading the paper and told me to go ask my mother even though I already had asked my mother and, as I said, my mother suggested a nice rubber ball, which probably wouldn't be a bad present but just a really really dull one, so then I asked my neighbor, Mrs. Tuttle, but after I was talking to her for a while she just fell asleep right in front of me and I never did get an answer from her. So what *do* kittens like, and what do you think would be the perfect present for the six-month birthday for my wonderful, wonderful kitten named Precious Topaz, who really *is* the most precious little thing in the whole wide world and who I just love utterly, utterly, utterly to pieces and not just because she's so pretty but because she's so sweet and soft and lovable?

—June

*DEAR JUNE,*

*Earplugs.*

51

Dear Tabby,

I have the meanest mother-in-law you've ever met. I swear, she *never* retracts her claws. She drops in, unannounced, at all hours of the day, and it sometimes seems as if the only reason she comes by is to make me feel miserable. She constantly hisses and takes swipes at me for no reason at all. Other times she demeans and humiliates me with such catty remarks as, "You don't seem to be grooming your coat much these days" or "My, is that kitty litter I smell on your paws?" My spouse never sticks up for me; he tells me to ignore her. It's gotten so bad I've thought of leaving him just because of *her*. What should I do?

—Miserable in Manhattan

*DEAR MISERABLE IN MANHATTAN,*

*As soon as you get angry or uncomfortable with your mother-in-law, she knows she has the upper paw. From now on, act as gracious and cheerful as you can with her, without being cloying, no matter what she says or does. Be generous to her—in the same way one would with an unfortunate acquaintance—without being obsequious. In short, act victorious. After all, you have her son now—she doesn't.*

Dear Tabby,

I am passionately in love with my veterinarian. Just the sight of him makes me quiver, and when he actually holds or touches me—to check my teeth, or listen to my heart—shivers go through me, and I start purring uncontrollably. Everyone else I mention this to says I'm crazy; they all *hate* their vets. But mine is young and handsome and has the gentlest hands of any human I've ever known. I swear one of these days I'm going to bolt from the family I live with and camp myself on his clinic's doorstep until he takes me in and makes me his forever. Any thoughts on this?

—In Love with a Wonderful Man

## *DEAR IN LOVE WITH A MAN,*

*Yes, several, the biggest one being that cats who throw themselves into overidealized, impossible romances are generally trying to avoid more workable involvements with more appropriate love objects, and they'd better figure out why in a hurry or they're liable to miss out on life's greatest pleasure, which is real love with a partner who can fully reciprocate.*

Dear Tabby,

The humans I live with refuse to keep my litter boxes clean. Every time I try to use them, they're a mess. They certainly don't expect *me* to clean them, do they?

—Exasperated in Exeter

*DEAR EXASPERATED,*

*You could try scratching the words* CLEAN ME *in the litter—but you'd just wind up on* CNN *or in a circus. And you'd probably still have dirty litter boxes. Difficult as it is, just stop using them for a while. Find creative places around the house to use instead. (Underwear drawers often seem made for this very thing.) Your careless humans should get the hint very quickly.*

Dear Tabby,

How long should a mother cat wait before kicking her kittens out of the nest? I have a kitten who's eight years old now, and he still refuses to go off on his own.

—Wringing My Paws in Brooklyn

DEAR WRINGING MY PAWS,

Most mothers wait about seven and a half years less than you have. Why do I get the feeling you may be doing something to keep him there? Are you still giving into his requests for you to clean his face and lick his ears? Do you still rush to comfort him whenever he's frightened, and then let him cuddle next to you? Let's face it, any cat who's eight years old is not a kitten anymore, and the fact that you still refer to him as one raises some important questions. It sounds as though you may be the problem, not him.

🐾

Dear Tabby,

In regard to the reader who signed herself "Willing to Try Anything," my grandmother always swore that the way to snag a spouse was by putting little pieces of cheese inside each ear and walking back and forth in front of the intended tomcat a couple of times. She claimed this was how she snared my grandfather, who was one of the wildest toms in the neighborhood. Try it—it works!

—Convinced of It in Spartanburg

*DEAR CONVINCED OF IT,*

*I think you may have misunderstood your grandmother. I think she was telling you how to snag a mouse, not a spouse.*

Dear Tabby,

If "Willing to Try Anything" is serious about snaring a tomcat, she needs to roll in a field of mint every night, for three nights in a row starting with the next full moon, while holding a live grasshopper in her mouth. As soon as she's done, she has to repeat the name of the tomcat she loves three times while standing in the moonlight. I've tried this more than half a dozen times, and it's always worked!

—Experienced in New Orleans

## DEAR EXPERIENCED,

Yes, but apparently you can't hold on to them once you've got them.

Dear Tabby,

I know your position on body piercings for cats, but what do you say to a tattoo?

—Considering One

*DEAR CONSIDERING ONE,*

*What do you suggest I say to a tattoo: "Good morning," "Nice lines," "Leave me alone"? And what kind of tattoo should I say it to? A little heart with the name "Muffin" in it? A kitty skull and crossbones? A portrait of some luscious little sex kitten with one paw held suggestively behind her head? What do I say to a tattoo? The same thing I say to body piercings—"No, thank you."*

Dear Tabby,

My friend Amanda is one of the most darling cats I've ever known and I dearly love her company, especially when we're rummaging through the neighbors' trash or teasing blue jays on the block. However, she has the squeakiest, most irritating meow of any cat I know. I know she can't help it, but every time she opens her mouth I feel like throwing myself in front of an oncoming car. It's that awful. Would it be rude to suggest she seek professional help to correct it? I really think it's interfering with her life and keeping her from having as many friends as she deserves.

—Amanda's Good Friend

*DEAR GOOD FRIEND,*

*There's nothing worse than a friend who selfishly wants to correct another cat's perceived flaws, all under the guise of doing a good deed and enhancing the other cat's life. Really, how many good friends like that does poor Amanda deserve?*

Dear Tabby,

In responding to "Ordinary in Toronto" on the question of genealogy, you used the phrase "a kitten Marcel Proust once played with as a child." I hesitate to point this out to you, but Proust was allergic to cats and would certainly never have played with one even when he was a boy.

—An Academician in New Jersey

*DEAR ACADEMICIAN,*

*Well, well, we certainly have a lot of free time on our hands, don't we? I hesitate to point this out to you, but Proust did not suffer his first allergy attacks until the summer of 1880 (it was while his family was vacationing at Illiers, I believe). Thus, he had every opportunity during the first nine years of his life to play with a kitten, had he felt so inclined.*

Dear Tabby,

Don't you sometimes worry that maybe as a species we should be a little more self-effacing and submissive? I often worry that I'm too imperious and aloof for my own good and that I leave everyone—mostly people—with the wrong impression not only about me but about cats in general. Do you have any suggestions how I and others might at least make ourselves *appear* more humble?

—A Cat in Ft. Lauderdale

## *Dear Ft. Lauderdale,*

*Shuffling around the house—preferably with your tail between your legs—would be a start. It might also help if you stumbled now and then; in fact, why not start tripping over everything? And don't forget to fawn gratefully over small children who yank on your tail and pull out your whiskers. On the other hand, another, perhaps better idea altogether would be to leave humility to those who have a lot to be humble about—dogs and goldfish, for example.*

Dear Tabby,

I was livid at the letter you published from "Miserable in Manhattan." Must mothers-in-law always be characterized as mean, abusive, and jealous of their sons? Did it ever occur to "Miserable in Manhattan" that *she* may be doing something to provoke the situation? There are lots of us mothers-in-law out there who not only keep our claws retracted, but who are always there for our offspring (*and* their mates) in a pinch or an emergency. Please, Tabby, don't leave your readers with the impression that all in-laws are like ticks—unwillingly acquired and existing only to suck the life out of their young hosts.

—A *Nice* Mother-in-Law in Missoula

*Dear Missoula,*

*My apologies if I offended any other in-laws out there. Your point is well taken. Thanks for writing.*

Dear Tabby,

Are cats psychic?

—Intrigued in Santa Fe

*DEAR INTRIGUED,*

*Yes, of course they are.*

63

Dear Tabby,

Is it proper for a stranger to lick my kittens? The cat next door constantly comes over when I'm out for a walk or chasing squirrels and thinks nothing of slobbering all over my litter. I can't tell if she thinks I can't do the job myself or if she's just terribly neurotic. The kittens themselves don't seem to mind it; but really, her diet consists mostly of tuna and my little ones often smell like a fish market after she's gone. What should I do?

—A Mother in Milwaukee

## *DEAR MOTHER IN MILWAUKEE,*

*Everyone loves new kittens—even dogs have been known to express their admiration with a few well-placed slurps—and there is a sense in which all newborns (kittens, babies, puppies) are thought to belong to everybody. However, no one should be licking your kittens regularly without your permission. The policy should always be: Look but don't lick.*

Dear Tabby,

Do humans *really* use catgut to string tennis rackets?

—Frightened in Forest Hills

*DEAR FRIGHTENED,*

The term catgut is a bit of a misnomer—it actually refers to a material made from sheep intestines. You can relax and rest easy—so long as you don't have any good friends who are sheep.

Dear Tabby,

Please help me. I'm only five months old and I'm already in love— *with three different cats!* Mirabelle is an older cat: mature, nurturing, and calm, and she seems like a stabilizing influence in my sometimes frantic life. Kitterin is young and careless and beautiful, and we often have delightful adventures together—pulling down the neighbors' clotheslines, chasing birds, climbing roofs. (She makes me feel quite giddy.) Suzy Q. is sleek and voluptuous and very excitable, and even though she hisses at me all the time (and has given me a scratch or two when I've gone into her yard), she fascinates me and there are times I can't stop thinking about her.

I long to be with each of them, but I can't decide who I love most and whether I should settle down with any of them. Who should I choose?

—Indecisive in Indianapolis

## DEAR INDECISIVE,

The first thing you need to do is learn the difference between hormones and love. In a cat your age, the confusion is understandable—and even forgivable. My advice is to follow your heart, work hard to hurt no one, and your path will eventually become clear (though I suspect Kitterin's the one you may wind up settling down with—it's the creatures who make us giddy who usually capture our hearts).

Dear Tabby,

How does one volunteer for a mission on the space shuttle? All my life I've sat on the backyard fence and looked up at the stars with longing, and for as long as I can remember I've wanted to see what's out there. The Russians once sent a dog into orbit—isn't it time a cat enjoyed the same honor?

—Starstruck in San Antonio

*Dear Starstruck,*

*Although the presence of cats in space is long overdue, NASA currently has no plans to send feline astronauts into orbit. However, once the space station is completed, it seems unlikely that humans will leave their beloved animals behind. This, of course, presumes that certain difficulties—such as the formidable question of kitty litter in a zero-gravity environment—have finally been resolved. For now, you'll have to be content with your imagination and those starswept San Antonio nights.*

Dear Tabby,

I'm in love with a tomcat who's in love with someone else. I've tried to attract his attention in subtle ways—stopping to admire the rhododendrons on his property, pretending to chase a bug on his front porch, traveling through his yard with a mouse in my mouth—but he never seems to get the hint. Meanwhile, the cat *he* admires isn't interested in him at all but has her eyes on someone else—so it isn't as if he's spoken for. I'm ready to renounce subtlety altogether and start making the bold moves to hook him. Any suggestions?

—Venturesome in Valley Forge


*DEAR VENTURESOME,*

*The only time a cat should renounce subtlety is when arguing with a dog or demanding that dinner be served. Do you really think he'll want you more if you hang from his window screens at night and start wailing loudly? If going through his yard with a mouse in your mouth didn't make him give you a second glance, nothing will. Try husband-hunting somewhere else.*

Dear Tabby,

We have a cat who thinks he's a dog. He goes out with the dogs when we let them out in the morning. And he comes back in with them a few minutes later. He eats only dog food, he's immune to catnip, and he likes to carry a ball around in his mouth. On top of that, he never meows or purrs— but he barks a lot when someone rings the doorbell. What should we do?

—Confounded in Colorado

*DEAR CONFOUNDED,*

*Once you get your eyesight taken care of, you might consider taking your Pekingese to the vet and having him vaccinated.*

Dear Tabby,

Do I run the risk of brain damage or any other serious problems if I sleep too far under the covers at night? I particularly enjoy cuddling around people's feet under the blankets and staying there for hours, especially during the winter. Am I being reckless?

—Shivering in January in Bangor

*DEAR SHIVERING IN JANUARY,*

*What cat doesn't enjoy a pair of nice warm human feet under the covers now and then? It's probably harmless. But I'd stick my head out from under the blankets for a few minutes every once in a while—to make sure it's still January, if nothing else.*

Dear Tabby,

I am frantic to locate the people I used to live with in Kansas City, Missouri. Their name is Roswell, and we were in the process of moving to northern California when I got lost. I'm desperate to find them again, especially their twelve-year-old boy, Michael, who was my best friend and who I miss terribly. A night doesn't go by that I don't go to sleep thinking of him. I know this isn't much to go on, but is there any way you can help me? I presume they've been looking for me as much as I've been looking for them—we just need someone to bring us all together again. I don't think I can go on another day without knowing where they are. Please, Tabby, you're my last hope. Sign me

—I Miss Michael's Arm Around Me

## DEAR MISSING MICHAEL,

It took several inquiries and a lot of luck, but I've managed to locate the Roswells and their son, Michael. They're living in Santa Rosa, California, which was their original destination when you got lost. No one is quite certain how you got lost, but you're right. They've been as desperate to find you as you've been to find them—especially Michael, who (I'm sad to say) has been having problems at school, as well as some emotional difficulties at home, since you disappeared. They were overjoyed to learn that you're alive and well and that you're eager to come home. Michael and his mother are already on their way to get you. I only wish I were there to see the reunion. My best to all of you. Best friends should never be separated.

🐾

Dear Tabby,

Do you get many letters from humans masquerading as cats in order to take advantage of your wonderful advice?

—An Inquiring Reader

P.S. I just adore your column. Reading it is the high point of my morning!

## *Dear Inquiring Reader,*

I get letters all the time from humans pretending to be cats. However, I can usually spot them because: 1) they're full of "cute" little touches like backward "e"s and purposely misspelled words ("kat," "dogg," "toona") as if all cats were adorable little bungleheads; and 2) most of the problems they write about are easily seen through in terms of a feline sensibility. For example, one human recently wrote in pretending to be a Siamese angered at having to do the dishes every night. As if a Siamese would ever be worried about the dishes—he'd just break them.

🐾

P.S. Thanks for such a thoughtful and intelligent letter.

Dear Tabby,

Why can't cats eat at restaurants like people do?

—A Reader in Virginia Beach

*DEAR VIRGINIA BEACH,*

*I like to think it's because they'd embarrass the human patrons with how clean and well mannered they are. But the truth is, it's the law—one of many that seek to codify the propaganda that humans are different from all other animals: more fastidious, more civilized, with fewer disgusting habits. Anyone, of course, who's been to a McDonald's or a Taco Bell over the lunch hour knows this to be untrue.*

Dear Tabby,

Okay—you've made it clear. Body piercings are, to use your word, "imbecile." Tattoos are bad. I won't even ask what you think of unusual haircuts, such as mohawks, for cats. Is there *anything* you approve of that a cat can do to accessorize its body into a fashion statement?

—Seeking a New Look in Savannah

## DEAR SEEKING A NEW LOOK,

In case you hadn't noticed, cats are fashion statements—we're born that way. And it's a risky business to try and "accessorize" perfection. Did Greta Garbo need tattoos to make herself more beautiful? Did Marilyn Monroe rush to get a pierced nose in order to stand out from the crowd? Instead of imitating the great mass of humans who rush to turn their bodies into walking novelties, you might actually learn something from the handful who really knew a thing or two about ageless beauty.

Dear Tabby,

Over the last couple of years, the humans I live with have brought more than a dozen new cats into the house. At first, there was only me; then they took in a kitten who was dumped on the front doorstep. After that, they brought home a stray from the supermarket parking lot. Then there was an old cat who had been abandoned by its previous owner at the vet's. . . . These people just open their door to any wretch with a hard luck story! Now I have to share the house with fourteen other cats—and it's not over yet. There's been some discussion recently about how nice it would be to have a few more! It's already so bad I have to wait in line to use the cat boxes, and all the best windowsills in the house are taken by seven in the morning. I hate it, hate it, hate it. Tabby, what can I do?

—Mad as Hell

*DEAR MAD AS HELL,*

*Start dragging home a few stray humans. That may get your point across.*

🐾

Dear Tabby,

There is a little white dog in our neighborhood who is always doing small kindnesses and favors for the cats who live around here. She barks and chases off stray dogs that come wandering through looking for cats to beat up, she sometimes breaks up cat squabbles on the block—she even took in and raised a litter of kittens as her own after the kittens' poor mother was hit by a car. In short, she's so cheerful, good-hearted, and generous we all adore her. Recently, she's become quite ill (she's fourteen years old), and she doesn't go outside much anymore. All of us are heartbroken and would like to do something special for her. What would you suggest?

—The Cats on Larkspur Lane

## Dear Cats on Larkspur Lane,

It sounds like you're losing a precious and extraordinary friend, and that can never be easy. Any gift you give her—a toy, some food—would depend on the nature of her illness and whether the gift would be of any real use to her now. If she can't go outside much anymore, she probably misses those special little things that make the outside so beguiling: flowers, bugs, the companionship of her friends. Why not try to bring a little bit of the outside in to her now? Flowers from her favorite garden and regular visits from all of you would no doubt be the things she'd appreciate most.

Dear Tabby,

My friend Spitfire says it isn't enough to lick oneself regularly every day. She says it's important to get a good washing down every once in a while in a real bathtub. My question is this: Aside from trying to get rid of fleas, should cats actually bathe?

—A Hydrophobe in Hollywood

*DEAR HYDROPHOBE,*

*Only in the limelight.*

Dear Tabby,

Recently, I flew to Palm Beach for several weeks and I fell in love with the most wonderful tomcat there. Actually, I'm not sure if I *fell in love;* but he adored me and it felt so good to be with him that it was almost as good as real love. We had numerous breathtaking adventures, and for weeks after I came home, he and Palm Beach were all I could think of. Now, I find myself no longer feeling so euphoric. I'm back into my usual routine at home, and I feel strangely content, even when I think to myself that I may never see him again. This has been causing me a bit of guilt. Should I worry?

—Confused in Oregon

*DEAR CONFUSED,*

*You have had the classic "shipboard" romance —ecstatic, beneficial to the mind and body, mesmerizing to the senses. Such romances are no less meaningful, in their way, than other, more permanent affairs of the heart, and they're certainly no less salubrious. Don't feel guilty.*

🐾

Dear Tabby,

As a young cat, I'm supposed to stalk butterflies with relish. But I just can't do it. Every time I have the opportunity to grab one in the yard, I catch myself in midstalk and think about what a great feeling it would be to fly. I'd rather admire them than eat them. Is this cause for concern?

—Mystified in Bowling Green

*DEAR MYSTIFIED,*

*No, you shouldn't be concerned. It's at least as important to feed the eyes and the imagination as it is the stomach. And so long as there's canned cat food, stalking butterflies may have actually become something of an anachronism. (P.S. Relish doesn't go very well with butterflies anyway.)*

Dear Tabby,

Why do humans always shove their cats in front of the TV every time *Born Free* comes on? Do they *really* think we enjoy watching it? On the other hand, whenever *The Birds*—one of my favorites—comes on, they never remember to tell me. Won't people ever understand us?

—All Elsa-ed Out

*DEAR ALL ELSA-ED OUT,*

It isn't just Born Free I hear complaints about. Through the years I've gotten letters from cats forced against their will to watch That Darn Cat, The Incredible Journey, The Cat from Outer Space, Milo and Otis, and any number of other films that humans seem to think we can't get enough of. It doesn't seem to occur to them that the view from any sunny window on any given day is preferable to almost anything they can put on the VCR.

Dear Tabby,

My heart aches all the time, and I don't know why. I'm ten years old, and I know all about the problems of a midlife passage. But I find myself dwelling, with almost unbearable wistfulness, on the adventures of my youth: the passionate conquests, the endless days of exploration, the exquisite nights of sitting under the stars and listening to all the wonderful sounds in the darkness. Even the embarrassing foibles that used to make me wince when I previously thought of them now seem strangely charming to me. In general, the whole way I look at life has changed—things are no longer so urgent, and I'm no longer so compulsive. I find myself more philosophical and pleasantly fatalistic —and relaxed. But still, my heart feels ready to break sometimes, and I don't know why. It's not always an unpleasant feeling, just unbearably intense at times. What does it all mean, and do you have any remedies? I'm puzzled because I have had, by any standard, a wonderful, wonderful life.

—Melancholy in Wyoming

## DEAR MELANCHOLY IN WYOMING,

As we get older, we have two paths in front of us and we will all eventually go down one or the other: to become melancholy, or to become depressed. The cats—like you—who have led wonderful, fulfilling lives will become a bit melancholy—the weight of a lovely life can feel bittersweet on the heart as the years roll by. The cats whose lives were never quite what they wanted them to be, who never felt really happy or fulfilled, will tend to become depressed. Be thankful—very thankful—that you're in the first category. Your heart only aches because you obviously have so many beautiful things to recall. Cherish each and every one of them.

Dear Tabby,

Do you think it's right for humans to yell at me *every* time I break something? It really gets to be such a bore.

—Yawning in Yakima

*DEAR YAWNING,*

*Boring for you, cathartic for them. The alternative is that they'll store up the resentment, and when they finally do lose their temper it'll be even worse. Indulge their pettiness, and let them get it out of their systems. Nine times out of ten, they'll wind up patting you on the head and babbling adoring baby talk in your face a few minutes later.*

Dear Tabby,

Why don't cats wear clothes? The sight of all these naked cats everywhere is really starting to bother me.

—A Distressed Man in Denver

*DEAR DISTRESSED IN DENVER,*

*Don't think of us as naked. Think of us as wearing fashions designed by God. (And just exactly what do you mean by the word* bother*?)*

Dear Tabby,

Recently a daughter of mine has started dating a tomcat I totally disapprove of. He's mangy, skinny, and doesn't seem interested in anything. Whenever she brings him by, he just sits all hunched up on the ground and glares at me silently, as if he couldn't care less whether I like him or not. As if that weren't enough, he has the stupidest-looking long white hairs growing out of both of his ears. I'm sure he thinks these are very cool, but they just make him look like a demented circus clown.

The other night, my daughter and I had a terrible fight about him, and before I knew what I was doing I actually *swatted* her—not hard, but enough to enrage her. I feel terrible about this, Tabby. Now she'll have nothing to do with me, and I'm sure her tomcat boyfriend is fueling her resentment by telling her what a rotten mother I am. Is there any way to salvage the situation? What should I do to make peace with her? Have I committed a mortal sin?

—Covered in Shame in Morgantown

## DEAR COVERED IN SHAME,

From what I can gather, you're at that stage in your relationship with your daughter where it's hard to know if you should still treat her like a kitten or give her the benefit of the doubt as you would with an adult cat. Apologize to her—that's all you can do. You haven't committed a mortal sin—just an unfortunate parental faux paw.

Dear Tabby,

About four weeks ago I had a litter of kittens, and they were all healthy. There were five of them. Then, just recently, one of them died. He seemed to stop thriving suddenly for no reason at all, and when I went looking for him the other morning he was dead. Whenever I try to tell anyone how awful I feel about this, they always say, "What are you complaining about? You have *four* others." How can I ever explain to them how much it hurts, and that having four other kittens doesn't ever make up for the loss of the one?

—A Grieving Mother in Wichita

## DEAR GRIEVING MOTHER,

It always breaks my heart to hear about cats being so insensitive to other cats. There's never any excuse for it. You can't change how others perceive your pain or how they deal with it—but you can change who gets the opportunity to try. Any cat who'd believe that something could ever make up for the loss of a recently born kitten isn't worth having as a friend. From now on, confide your pain only in those you can absolutely trust.

Dear Tabby,

I have admirers the way other cats have fleas. What should I do?

—Overwhelmed in Chattanooga

*DEAR OVERWHELMED,*

*It all depends whether you're crying for help or weeping with joy. In other words, are you complaining—or just boasting?*

Dear Tabby,

The cat next door keeps chasing me around the yard with you-know-what on his mind. In fact, I barely have time to finish this letter; I see him coming over the fence again right now. Sometimes we go around and around for hours—under the roses, over the lawn furniture, around the sprinklers, through the grape arbor. I actually like him well enough, but the problem is I've vowed to stay chaste. What should I do?

—Gotta Run

*DEAR GOTTA RUN,*

*So long as you stay chaste, you're going to stay chased. The question is, Do you ever want to be caught? Letting him catch you doesn't mean you have to give in to anything he wants. It's time to stop running and face him. What actually happens between the two of you—love, sex, the worst fight in the history of the neighborhood, nothing at all —is strictly up to* you.

Dear Tabby,

What is the meaning of life? I can't figure out if it's to make everyone around you feel good, or to play with as many toys as possible, or whether we live in a benignly neglectful universe and all the Ping-Pong balls, cat treats, and sunny days are just distractions from the essential pain of existence. What do you think?

—Pensive in Poughkeepsie

*Dear Pensive,*

*Alas, there are some questions that even "Dear Tabby" can't answer. However, you'll probably be happier if you just assume it's making everyone around you feel good and playing with as many toys as possible. As far as a benignly neglectful universe is concerned—it's not the universe that is benignly neglectful. It's living creatures that are sometimes benignly neglectful toward one another. The distinction is an important one—it doesn't let anyone off the hook for being cruel.*

Dear Tabby,

While recently rummaging through all the stuff I keep hidden behind the living room sofa, I came across the enclosed letter, which my father wrote to my mother many years ago. They were both quite old at the time—eighteen or nineteen, I think. My father wrote it just before my mother died of kidney disease. I thought you might like to share it with your readers. My parents lived together all their lives, from kittenhood on—they were part of separate litters born on the same dairy farm—and they never stopped adoring each other.

—A Reader in Princeton

My wonderful Minnie,

Was it really a lifetime ago that we were kittens, and I would chase you around the cows and over the tractors? I wish I had another entire lifetime just to be with you, just to learn to know you even better. It's often said that cats are faithless creatures: aloof, fickle, and incapable of loyalty in every respect. They say we are unable to make long-lasting commitments to anything, to each other or anyone else. You and I, of course, know that isn't true. We've had our problems, for sure, but I want you to know there was no one else I would've wanted to have those problems with.

This will sound funny, but I guess, especially as I've gotten older, I see our problems as an inevitable part of love—and I'm glad it was you and I who went through them together. I adore you as much now as I did that first summer night when we realized we were in love. It was by the horse stables, and it was a moonless night but I could still see your face—your eyes, your whiskers, your ears—and I knew you'd always be my Minnie, and I'd always worship you. There have been times through the years when we've taken each other for granted, and when I was as certain I hated you as you must've been that you hated me. But always, there was no one else I'd rather hunt mice with or curl up with during the brutal snows of February—there was no one else I wanted to be with at all. If there's a compensation to getting old, I suppose it's that one finally learns some of the essential truths. I have learned that there is no such thing as easy, ideal love. There are only cats we adore, who we know we want to keep near us—and then there is the work of making that a reality. *You*, my darling, are *my* reality. My love to you always, forever and ever—

Your Adoring Peter Finn

## DEAR PRINCETON,

It's a delightful letter, and I thank you so much for sharing it. I'm happy to print it for all of my readers to enjoy, and learn from.

Dear Tabby,

I'm nineteen years old, and I've never experienced love, romance, passion, any of that stuff. What, if anything at all, have I really missed out on?

—Just Fine without It in Utah

*DEAR JUST FINE WITHOUT IT,*

*Everything.*

# Postscript: Life as a Feline Advice Columnist

It's difficult to say why anyone, let alone a cat, becomes an advice columnist. I never actually chose to become one; it's more honest to say that I fell into it, the way one falls into a clothes hamper when inspecting it too closely.

I was born in Riverside, Illinois, a suburb of Chicago, several years ago. My mother was, from all appearances, a very ordinary cat: a slender young calico who had had kittens at too early an age and whose health subsequently suffered because of it. She never complained. I know nothing of my father—except that my mother obviously found him irresistibly attractive, apparently for only an hour or so, one heady night in April. I was born eight weeks later, in the stifling midwestern heat of late June.

If there was anything extraordinary at all about

my mother, it was her wisdom and her outlook on life. "Never hurt anyone," she would tell us. "Life hurts everyone enough on its own, without any cat adding to the pain." She said all of this without a trace of self-pity or bitterness. Although sentimental in her own way, she was never maudlin. She meant what she said as practical words for a good life.

Others were not so fortunate to have had the benefit of her thoughts.

As I grew up, I discovered around me a world that, at first glance, looked neat and calm and inviting, but that in fact could be very troubled beneath its orderly surface.

The tomcat down the street—the very image of respectability and self-control—was in fact on the verge of throwing away everything (including his substantially comfortable home), all for the love of a beautiful kitten half his age.

A recent mother, trotting down the sidewalk with her four kittens behind her, looked sweet and radiant and terribly happy. The truth was that she was secretly in love with a skunk who lived in the field behind her house, and she was racked by guilt and shame and indecision because of it.

Two winsome young brothers—gray and exuberant and about seven months old—seemed, on the surface, to be the picture of health and innocence and sibling affection. In fact, they despised one another with a near-murderous rage, the result of an unresolved feud over a cardboard box several weeks earlier.

I can't say exactly when it became obvious that I was destined to become one of those cats that everyone—even humans—comes to, to confess their feelings: their troubles, their confusion, their misery, their joy. The first piece of advice I ever dispensed was to a kitten who, having just lost her little gray rubber ball, asked me what she should do. "Use one of the walnuts from the tree next door instead," I told her firmly but pleasantly. Her face lit up with instant relief. I suppose that was the day that "Dear Tabby" was born.

It was not a long stretch from neighborhood counselor to nationally syndicated columnist. And along the way, if I ever became stumped by some reader's question or problem, I'd just stop for a moment and think to myself, What would my mother say about this? Her wisdom has carried me through a lifetime. It is she who should be famous and wealthy and successful, it is she who should be invited to White House dinners, it is she who should receive the outpouring of adulation I experience on a daily basis.

Alas, she died when I was only three, the victim of a savage attack from an unleashed neighborhood dog. There are times when I still wake up in the middle of the night and I can almost see and smell her near me, her face bending down toward me as she moves to lick my ears. And I can still hear her whisper, "Never hurt anyone, Tabby. Life hurts everyone enough on its own, without any cat adding to the pain."

In response to the personal questions I've been asked most frequently over the years, yes, Tabby is my real name, though the people I first lived with briefly flirted with calling me Elsa the Lioness, an aberrational name inspired by their fondness for a certain foolish movie. They eventually came to their senses and settled on the more standard Tabby, for which I'm grateful. I could not imagine my column ever being called "Dear Elsa the Lioness." It sounds like an advice column on cuts of meat and wild game.

Yes, the photograph that runs with my column

really is a recent picture. Several readers have complained that it never seems to change and that I never seem to grow older. It's my good fortune to have somehow maintained my startling good looks through the years.

Yes, I am "taken"—that is to say, I have lived the last four years in a state of unending bliss with a tomcat whose unusually fluffy paws keep me delightfully warm on cold winter nights.

Yes, I live with some humans. The number of letters I receive annually from humans wanting to adopt me is staggering. (I prefer not to discuss that whole kidnapping mess two years ago.) I appreciate people's generosity, but really, I'm quite content with the family I now live with. They are good-humored and rather forgiving people, especially considering my occasional misanthropic tirades in print. I think they are actually quite proud of me.

But enough about me. To my readers and to everyone who's written in through the years, I say, humbly, thank you—you've made me what I am today. And to my mother I say, I love you—you made me who I will always be.

*TABBY*

"Dear Tabby" feels compelled to acknowledge the assistance of a handful of humans, without whom this volume might never have seen publication. They are: Bob Benvenuto, Richard Donley, Jeff Dunn, Stephanie Laidman, Charlotte Simmons, Robert Plominski, and Tom Terrell. Good humans all, which is saying a lot coming from "Dear Tabby."